The City Mouse &
The Country Mouse

© Sigal Adler
No part of this publication may be reproduced, photocopied, translated, stored in a database or
Distributing any form or by any means (electronic, optical or mechanical, including photocopying or recording)
without prior written permission of the author.

Once upon a time, there were two cousin mice,

Both family and friends, which is just as nice.

A gray country mouse, cheery and kind.

The best sort of mouse you can find.

But his cousin mouse, plump and witty,

Lived richly in the big house in the city.

One early morning, as the sun shone bright,
the city mouse awoke after a good night.
He had slept well, but something was wrong,
All that city noise! Oh, it was far too strong!

"I need some rest and sun," he thought,
"I'll visit the country; I'll like it a lot."
He called his cousin, "I'll be on my way,
this weekend no less, I'm coming to stay!"

The country mouse was thrilled, and justly so,
He last met his cousin quite some time ago.
While he was happy, he was embarrassed too;
his house was old and tiny, what would he do?

Soon his city cousin would come for some rest.
So he decided he would surprise his city guest;
with a meal so delicious he'd lick his plate,
his house is tiny, but the food would be great!

He crept to the kitchen and stole some cheese,

Then he grabbed pieces of ham with great ease.

He picked three oranges right off the tree,

and a couple of nuts: what a feast it would be!

As the weekend approached, the very next day,

The rich city mouse rode the train on his way.

As he arrived, he looked around with a frown:

"It's so tiny, nothing like my house uptown."

But the country mouse was very forgiving,

he didn't mind, he liked his way of living.

They were best friends, they would never fight

Though the city mouse was not so polite.

They sat hungry by the table, ready to eat.

The table was packed with every kind of treat.

But the city mouse just sat with a pout.

He grumbled and pulled up his snout.

Though the meal was prepared with great love and care,
The city mouse nibbled some bits here and there.
A crumb of cheese and just a bite from the ham,
he was very displeased; this meal was a sham!

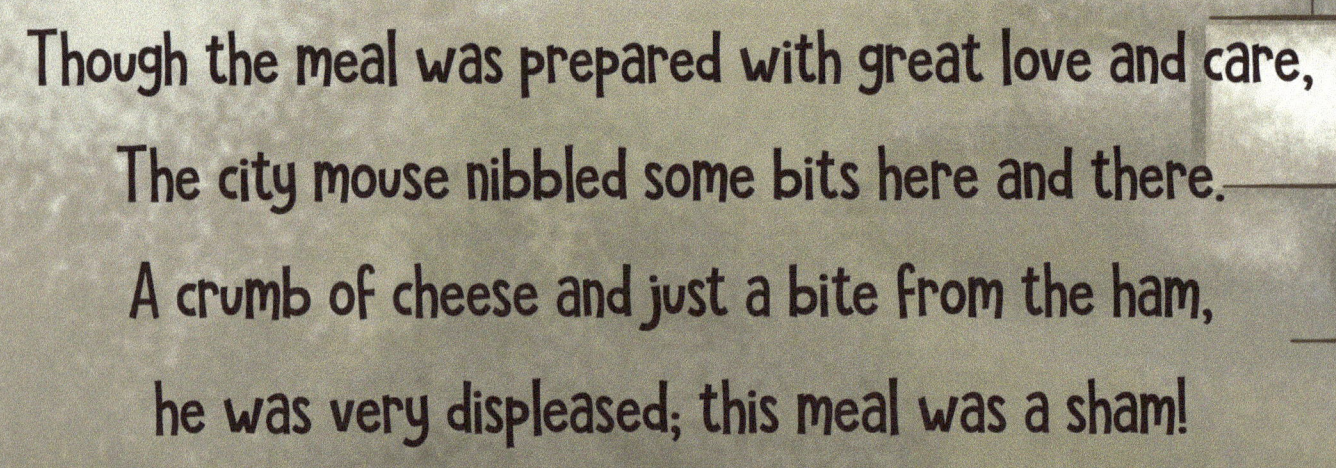

When they had finished, and the plates were all clear,
he looked at his cousin, and said with a sneer:
"I live in the city, with riches and charm,
You live in a small smelly country farm."

"In the city," he said, "there's much fun to be had,
the country is boring, so dreary and sad.
Come to the city, come visit me please,
We'll see every site; we'll taste every cheese!"

Hearing that, the country mouse was intrigued,

he'd never been to the city, now he'd visit it indeed.

Setting off on the road, without giving it thought,

Perhaps he was wrong, and his cousin was not?

The mice spent the day together, until the sun set.

"This bed is too hard," the city mouse said, upset.

Tomorrow they would take the train and go

to visit the city, where the bright lights glow.

After traveling all day, they arrived quite late,
they jumped off the train, walked through the gate.
The city night was quiet, there wasn't a sound,
So the country mouse squinted and looked all around.

The rich city mouse had a house that was grand,
Filled with every luxury a mouse could demand.
"See, cousin, isn't it great?" the city mouse said,
The country mouse saw and nodded his head.

Since they were hungry, they decided to dine,
the table was packed, it all seemed so fine.
There were wonderful cakes, glazed and sweet
and even a silky rug spread under their feet.

As he sat on a pillow, his heart skipped a beat,
there was so much to try, there was so much to eat.
Delicious soft pastries, berries and whipped cream,
The country food he'd served, how poor did it seem!

The country mouse couldn't believe his eyes,
there was a heap of fruits and a mountain of pies.
This was all too much, his head then spun
he missed his own house; that's it - he was done.

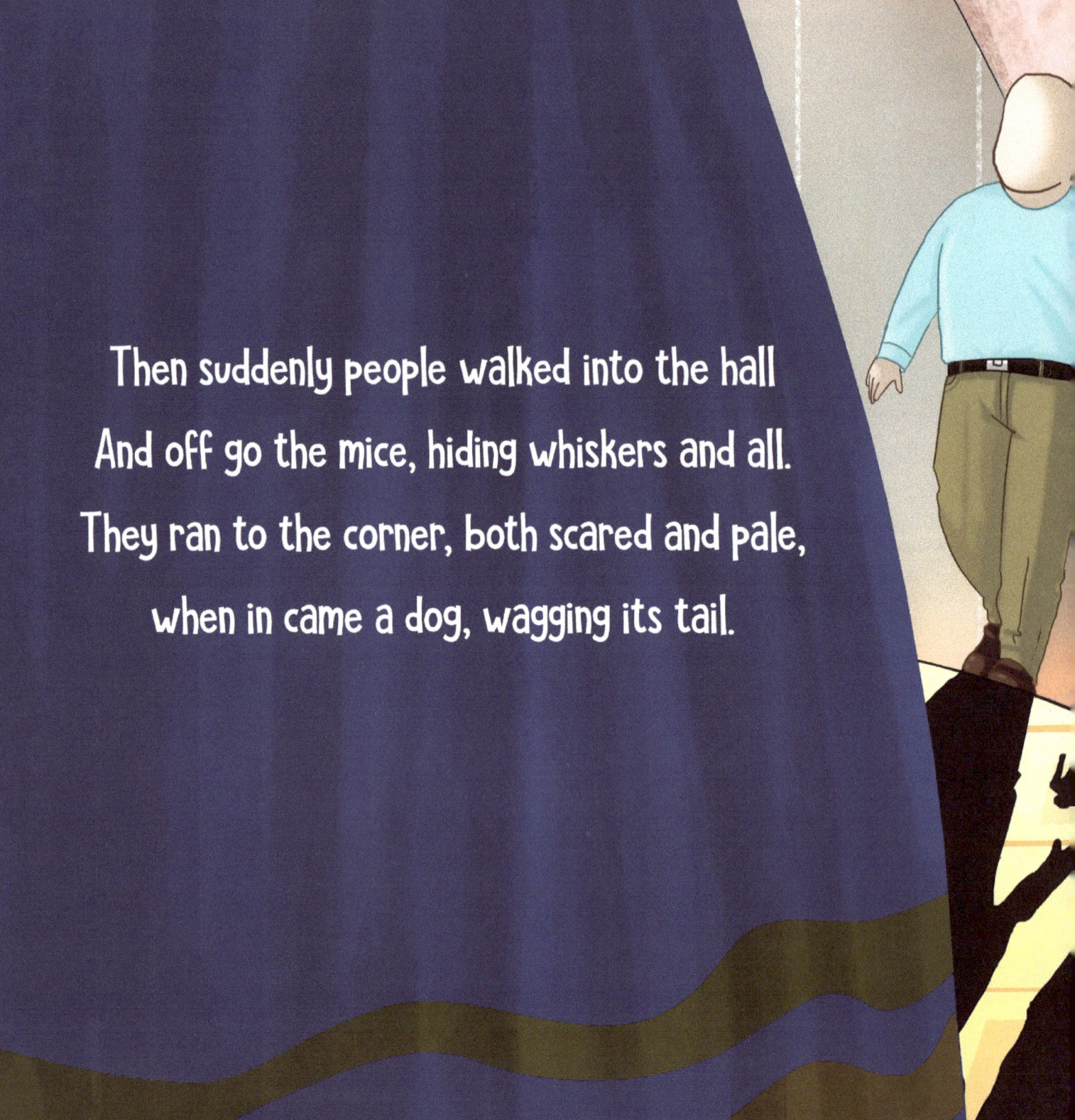

Then suddenly people walked into the hall
And off go the mice, hiding whiskers and all.
They ran to the corner, both scared and pale,
when in came a dog, wagging its tail.

Trapped in the corner, they could barely move a hair,
while the people were here, neither would dare.
When the food was done, the mice finally breathed,
though they were safe, they weren't relieved.

Then the country mouse said to his city cousin,
"Though you are rich with cakes by the dozen,
with chef-made meals and a soft carpet too,
I would not want to live here if I were you.

You see, people and mice just don't get along,
What good is your wealth if you do not belong?"
The country mouse explained, "I'd rather be healthy,
Better to be safe and sound than being wealthy."

"Thank you so much," the country mouse smiled,
"Though the city is grand, it is rather wild.
I miss my home, where life is simple and slow,
I don't need all of this, it's time that I go."

After hugging goodbye, the mice surely knew,

They learned a big lesson, that much is true:

Even great wealth cannot buy you bliss;

One prefers that, the other wants this.

Whether you're a person or a country mouse,

we each like our own kind of house.

www.ingramcontent.com/pod-product-compliance
Lightning Source LLC
Chambersburg PA
CBHW041217240426
43661CB00012B/1072